RETAIL BUSINESSES MADE EASY

JUNE 5, 2023
ANOTHER INCREDIBLE BOOK WRITTEN WITH THE AI
ASSISTANCE OF
GENERAIT.NET

Table of Contents

CHAPTER 1: INTRODUCTION 6

CHAPTER 2: UNDERSTANDING RETAIL BUSINESSES 7

CHAPTER 3: CHOOSING THE RIGHT RETAIL BUSINESS 8

  IDENTIFY YOUR SKILLS AND EXPERTISE 8
  CONSIDER YOUR BUDGET AND LOCATION 9
  RESEARCH MARKET TRENDS 9
  ASSESS YOUR RISK TOLERANCE 9
  CONCLUSION 10

CHAPTER 4: CREATING A BUSINESS PLAN 10

  EXECUTIVE SUMMARY 10
  BUSINESS DESCRIPTION 11
  MARKET ANALYSIS 11
  PRODUCTS AND SERVICES 11
  MARKETING AND SALES STRATEGY 12
  OPERATIONS 12
  FINANCIAL PLAN 12

CHAPTER 5: FINANCING YOUR BUSINESS 13

  BOOTSTRAPPING 13
  SMALL BUSINESS LOANS 13
  INVESTORS AND PARTNERSHIPS 14
  CROWDFUNDING 14
  CONCLUSION 14

CHAPTER 6: REGISTERING YOUR BUSINESS 15

  BUSINESS STRUCTURE 15
  NAME AND BUSINESS REGISTRATION 15
  FEDERAL TAX IDENTIFICATION NUMBER 16
  OTHER BUSINESS REGISTRATIONS 16

CHAPTER 7: ACQUIRING PERMITS, LICENSES, AND CERTIFICATIONS 17

- Permits 17
- Licenses 18
- Certifications 18

CHAPTER 8: LOCATION AND LEASE NEGOTIATIONS 19

- Factors to Consider when Choosing a Location 19
  - 1. Foot Traffic 20
  - 2. Demographics 20
  - 3. Accessibility and Parking 20
  - 4. Competition 20
- Negotiating a Lease 21
  - 1. Understand your Expenses 21
  - 2. Negotiate the Rent 21
  - 3. Review the Lease Carefully 21
  - 4. Seek Legal Advice 22

CHAPTER 9: STORE DESIGN AND LAYOUT 22

- Customer Flow 22
- Merchandise Display 23
- Lighting 24

CHAPTER 10: INVENTORY MANAGEMENT 25

- Subchapter 10.1: Determining Inventory Needs 26
- Subchapter 10.2: Monitoring and Controlling Stock Levels 26
- Subchapter 10.3: Forecasting Sales and Trends 27
- Subchapter 10.1: Determining Inventory Needs 28
  - Product demand 28
  - Lead time 29
  - Sales history 29
  - Storage capacity 30
  - Budget and cash flow 30
  - Conclusion 30

SUBCHAPTER 10.2: MONITORING AND CONTROLLING STOCK LEVELS 31
SUBCHAPTER 10.3: FORECASTING SALES AND TRENDS 33

CHAPTER 11: HIRING AND TRAINING STAFF 35

SUBCHAPTER 11.1: RECRUITING AND INTERVIEWING CANDIDATES 35
SUBCHAPTER 11.2: ONBOARDING AND ORIENTATION 36
SUBCHAPTER 11.3: TRAINING AND DEVELOPMENT 37
SUBCHAPTER 11.1: RECRUITING AND INTERVIEWING CANDIDATES 38
    Defining Job Descriptions and Requirements *39*
    Posting Job Openings *39*
    Screening Resumes *40*
    Conducting Interviews *40*
    Checking References *41*
    Making the Hiring Decision *41*
SUBCHAPTER 11.2: ONBOARDING AND ORIENTATION 42
SUBCHAPTER 11.3: TRAINING AND DEVELOPMENT 44

CHAPTER 12: MARKETING AND ADVERTISING 46

DEFINING YOUR TARGET MARKET 47
DEVELOPING A MARKETING STRATEGY 47
TRADITIONAL ADVERTISING METHODS 48
DIGITAL MARKETING STRATEGIES 48
CONCLUSION 49
SUBCHAPTER 12.1: DEFINING YOUR TARGET MARKET 49
SUBCHAPTER 12.2: DEVELOPING A MARKETING STRATEGY 51
SUBCHAPTER 12.3: TRADITIONAL ADVERTISING METHODS 53
    Newspaper Ads *53*
    Direct Mail *54*
    Radio Ads *54*
    TV Ads *54*
SUBCHAPTER 12.4: DIGITAL MARKETING STRATEGIES 55
    Social Media Marketing: *56*
    Email Marketing: *56*
    Content Marketing: *56*
    Search Engine Optimization (SEO): *57*

Pay-Per-Click (PPC) Advertising: 57
Affiliate Marketing: 57

CHAPTER 13: SALES TECHNIQUES **58**

SUBCHAPTER 13.1: SALES SKILLS AND STRATEGIES 58
SUBCHAPTER 13.2: HANDLING CUSTOMER COMPLAINTS AND CHALLENGES . 59
SUBCHAPTER 13.3: UPSELLING AND CROSS-SELLING TECHNIQUES 60
CONCLUSION 60
SUBCHAPTER 13.1: SALES SKILLS AND STRATEGIES 61
Listening Skills 61
Product Knowledge 62
Customer Empathy 62
Effective Communication 62
Selling Techniques 63
Closing the Deal 63
SUBCHAPTER 13.2: HANDLING CUSTOMER COMPLAINTS AND CHALLENGES . 64

CHAPTER 14: MANAGING BUSINESS FINANCES **66**

BUDGETING AND FORECASTING 66
BOOKKEEPING AND ACCOUNTING 67
FINANCIAL PERFORMANCE ANALYSIS 68
CONCLUSION 68
SUBCHAPTER 14.1: BUDGETING AND FORECASTING 69
SUBCHAPTER 14.2: BOOKKEEPING AND ACCOUNTING 70
SUBCHAPTER 14.3: FINANCIAL PERFORMANCE ANALYSIS 72

CHAPTER 15: SCALING YOUR BUSINESS **74**

SUBCHAPTER 15.1: GROWING YOUR CUSTOMER BASE 74
SUBCHAPTER 15.2: EXPANDING YOUR PRODUCT OR SERVICE OFFERINGS 75
SUBCHAPTER 15.3: FRANCHISING AND LICENSING 76
SUBCHAPTER 15.1: GROWING YOUR CUSTOMER BASE 77
1. Focus on Customer Service 77
2. Offer Promotions and Discounts 78
3. Use Social Media Marketing 78
4. Attend Networking Events 79

5. Collect Customer Feedback..79
SUBCHAPTER 15.2: EXPANDING YOUR PRODUCT OR SERVICE OFFERINGS....80
   1. Analyze Your Current Offerings 80
   2. Research Trends and Competitors 81
   3. Modify Current Offerings..81
   4. Consider Bundling...82
   5. Partner with Other Businesses..82
   6. Keep Your Brand Image Consistent 82
SUBCHAPTER 15.3: FRANCHISING AND LICENSING 83

CHAPTER 16: CONCLUSION AND NEXT STEPS..................................85
NEXT STEPS 86

Chapter 1: Introduction

Welcome to *Retail Businesses Made Easy*! In this book, we will guide you through all the crucial steps to successfully operate a retail business. Whether you are a first-time entrepreneur or an experienced business owner, this book will provide you with valuable insights to take your retail business to the next level.

Retail businesses are an essential part of our economy and play a vital role in connecting customers with the products they need. A well-run retail business requires a combination of careful planning, hard work, and a deep understanding of the industry.

In this book, we will cover topics ranging from understanding the retail industry, choosing the right retail business, creating a business plan, financing your business, registering your business, acquiring permits and licenses, location and lease negotiations, store design and layout, inventory management, hiring and training staff, marketing and advertising, sales techniques, managing business finances, and scaling your business.

We designed this book to help you navigate the complex world of retail businesses. This book will provide you with the tools you need to succeed in the retail industry, no matter what type of retail business you are interested in starting or operating.

We are confident that this book will be an invaluable resource for you on your journey to create a successful retail business. Let's dive in!

Chapter 2: Understanding Retail Businesses

Retail is the process of selling consumer goods or services to customers through various channels of distribution to earn a profit. Retail businesses can take many forms, including brick and mortar stores, online storefronts, and mobile vendors.

One of the main components of a successful retail business is understanding the consumer market. Understanding the behavior and needs of customers is critical to creating a strategy that will drive sales and build customer loyalty. Researching what customers want and how they behave is a challenging but necessary aspect of building a profitable retail business.

In addition to consumer behavior, competition plays a crucial role in the success of retail businesses. Understanding the competition in the market can help businesses differentiate themselves and identify potential opportunities. Competition includes both direct competitors selling similar products and indirect competitors that may offer substitute products or services.

Another critical component of retail businesses is supply chain management. Managing the supply chain involves processes such as sourcing, logistics, inventory management, and supply chain optimization. The effective management of the supply chain can lead to lower costs, better quality products, and higher customer satisfaction.

Finally, technology is a crucial factor in the retail sector. The use of technology can help businesses automate processes, manage inventory, and analyze sales data. By leveraging technology, retail businesses can gain a competitive advantage and improve efficiency and profitability.

Overall, understanding the nature of retail businesses is key to creating and maintaining a successful retail business. Whether it be knowing the consumer market, analyzing competition, managing the supply chain, or leveraging technology, each component plays a critical role in building a profitable retail business.

Chapter 3: Choosing the Right Retail Business

Starting a retail business is an exciting and potentially lucrative venture, but it's important to choose the right type of retail business for your skills, interests, budget, and location. In this chapter, we'll cover some of the main factors to consider when choosing the right retail business for you.

IDENTIFY YOUR SKILLS AND EXPERTISE

The first step to choosing the right retail business is to evaluate your skills and expertise. Do you have experience in a particular industry or type of business? Do you have a passion for fashion, technology, or home decor? Identifying your areas of strength can help you narrow down your options and select a retail business that aligns with your knowledge, skills, and interests.

CONSIDER YOUR BUDGET AND LOCATION

Another important factor to consider when choosing a retail business is your budget and location. Depending on the type of business you choose, the cost of startup can vary significantly. A brick-and-mortar store will require a larger initial investment than an online store, for example. Location is also critical because you'll want to choose a high-traffic area that's accessible to your target customers.

RESEARCH MARKET TRENDS

It's important to research market trends to ensure that there is a demand for the type of retail business you're considering. Look for reports on consumer behavior and spending habits, as well as industry news and updates, to get a sense of how your business might perform in the current market. Consider the competition in the area and whether there is room for your business to differentiate itself and succeed.

ASSESS YOUR RISK TOLERANCE

Starting any type of business involves risk, but some types of retail businesses may be riskier than others. For example, a niche boutique that sells high-end products may have a smaller customer base and may be more vulnerable to economic downturns than a discount store that offers a wide range of affordable items. Assess your personal risk tolerance and consider factors such as supply chain disruptions, market volatility, and customer demand before making a final decision.

CONCLUSION

Choosing the right retail business is a crucial step in starting a successful venture. By taking into account your skills and expertise, budget and location, market trends, and risk tolerance, you can narrow down your options and select a business that is well-positioned for success.

Chapter 4: Creating a Business Plan

A solid business plan is the foundation of any successful retail business. It is the roadmap that will guide you through every step of starting and running your business. Here are some key elements that you should include in your business plan:

EXECUTIVE SUMMARY

Your executive summary is the first section of your business plan and should provide a brief overview of your entire plan. It should explain what your business will do, who your target market is, and what your goals are. Keep it concise and to the point.

BUSINESS DESCRIPTION

In this section, you should provide a more detailed description of your business. This should include your business name, location, mission statement, and goals. You should also explain why you believe there is a need for your business in the market and how you plan to meet that need.

MARKET ANALYSIS

Your market analysis should provide research and data about your target market, competitors, and industry trends. You should explain who your ideal customers are, what their buying habits are, and what motivates them to make a purchase. You should also analyze your competitors, their strengths and weaknesses, and how you plan to differentiate yourself from them.

PRODUCTS AND SERVICES

In this section, you should provide a detailed description of the products or services that your business will offer. Explain how your products or services will meet the needs of your target market and how you plan to source or create them.

MARKETING AND SALES STRATEGY

Describe how you plan to market your products or services to your target market. This should include details about your branding, advertising, and sales strategy. Be specific about how you plan to reach your customers and what tactics you will use to drive sales.

OPERATIONS

This section should explain how your business will operate day-to-day. It should detail your suppliers, production process, inventory management, and other logistics. Be sure to also include information about the legal structure of your business, any permits or licenses required, and the costs associated with operating your business.

FINANCIAL PLAN

Your financial plan should include your startup costs, revenue projections, and financial statements. This section will show how much money you need to start your business, where you will get funding, and how you plan to reach profitability. Be realistic in your projections and include a contingency plan for any unexpected financial issues.

A solid business plan takes time and effort to create, but it's a necessary step in order to set your business up for success. It will help you stay focused, make informed decisions, and give potential investors or lenders the information they need to support your business.

Chapter 5: Financing Your Business

Starting a retail business requires a considerable amount of funding, and choosing the right financing option is crucial to the success of your venture. There are several ways to fund your retail business, and it's important to evaluate each option carefully to determine which one is right for you.

BOOTSTRAPPING

Bootstrapping refers to starting and growing your business using only your personal finances or the business's profits.

While bootstrapping can be a viable option for some entrepreneurs, it can also be limiting in terms of growth potential since it relies solely on your financial resources. If you plan on launching a larger retail store, it may be necessary to seek other forms of financing.

SMALL BUSINESS LOANS

Small business loans are a popular financing option for many retail businesses. These loans can come from traditional banks, credit unions, or other lenders. To secure a small business loan, you will need to have a solid business plan in place, good credit, and a plan for repayment. While small business loans can be a good option for those who qualify, the application process can be lengthy and require a lot of documentation.

INVESTORS AND PARTNERSHIPS

Another financing option for retail businesses is to seek out investors or partnerships. This can involve selling percentages of the business or entering into a joint venture with another company or individual. It's important to carefully consider the terms of these types of arrangements and ensure that you are comfortable sharing control of your business.

CROWDFUNDING

Crowdfunding is a popular financing option that involves raising money from a large number of people typically through online platforms. This can be a good way to generate capital for your retail business, but it requires a strong marketing strategy and a compelling pitch to convince people to invest in your venture.

CONCLUSION

Financing your retail business requires careful consideration and evaluation of your options. Whether you choose to bootstrap, seek a small business loan, bring on investors or partners, or use crowdfunding, it's important to understand the pros and cons of each option and choose the one that best fits your needs and goals.

Chapter 6: Registering Your Business

Once you have decided on the type of retail business you want to start, the next step is to register your business with the appropriate government agencies. Registering your business is critical, as it makes your business a legal entity and enables you to apply for necessary licenses and permits.

BUSINESS STRUCTURE

Before you register your business, you need to decide on the structure of your business. There are several types of business structures including sole proprietorship, partnerships, corporations, and limited liability companies (LLCs). Each structure has its own advantages and disadvantages. It is recommended that you consult with a legal or financial advisor on which structure is best for your retail business.

NAME AND BUSINESS REGISTRATION

Once you have decided on the structure of your business, you need to choose a name for your business. The name should be unique and reflective of your brand. You should also check if the name is available and not already taken by another business.

After you have chosen a name, you need to register your business with the appropriate state agency. The process of registering your business varies depending on the state where you are located. Generally, you will need to fill out the necessary forms, pay the registration fee, and provide proof of identification and business structure.

FEDERAL TAX IDENTIFICATION NUMBER

After registering your business with the state, you need to apply for a Federal Tax Identification Number or Employer Identification Number (EIN) with the Internal Revenue Service (IRS). An EIN is a unique nine-digit number assigned to your business for tax purposes. You will need an EIN to open a business bank account, file taxes, and hire employees. You can apply for an EIN online with the IRS.

OTHER BUSINESS REGISTRATIONS

Depending on the nature of your business, you may need to register for other permits and licenses, such as a sales tax permit, zoning permit, or health permit. These registrations vary by state and city, so it is essential to check with your local government agencies to ensure that you are compliant with all regulations and requirements.

Registering your business can be a complex process, but it is a critical step in establishing your retail business. By registering your business, you can protect your personal assets and comply with all legal and regulatory requirements.

Chapter 7: Acquiring Permits, Licenses, and Certifications

Starting a retail business requires more than just a great product or service. You will also need to obtain various permits, licenses, and certifications before you can legally operate your business. These requirements vary by state and industry, so it's important to research and understand what is needed for your specific business.

PERMITS

Permits are typically required at the local level and may include things like zoning permits, building permits, and health permits. Zoning permits ensure that your business is located in a properly zoned area, while building permits ensure that any construction or alteration to your business location is up to code. Health permits are required for businesses that sell food or beverages and ensure that your establishment is clean and meets health and safety standards.

Be sure to contact your local government offices to determine what permits are required for your retail business. Keep in mind that obtaining permits can take time, so plan accordingly and factor in additional time for obtaining necessary approvals.

LICENSES

Licenses are typically required at the state level and may include things like sales tax licenses, employer identification numbers, and retail licenses. Sales tax licenses are required for businesses that plan to collect and remit sales tax in the state where they operate. Employer identification numbers, or EINs, are issued by the IRS and are used to identify your business for tax purposes. Retail licenses may be required for specific industries, such as alcohol sales or firearm sales.

Again, research what licenses are required for your retail business in your specific state. It is important to obtain all necessary licenses before operating your business, as failure to do so can result in penalties and fines.

CERTIFICATIONS

Certifications may also be required for certain industries, such as organic or fair trade certifications for businesses that sell natural or specialty products. These types of certifications indicate that your business is meeting certain standards and can be a selling point for consumers who are concerned with social or environmental responsibility.

Research what certifications are available for your industry and consider obtaining them if they are relevant to your business. These certifications can help differentiate your business from competitors and attract socially and environmentally conscious consumers.

Overall, obtaining the necessary permits, licenses, and certifications may seem daunting, but it is a critical step in legally operating a retail business. Consult the appropriate government agencies and industry organizations to ensure that you are meeting all requirements and can focus on growing a successful business.

Chapter 8: Location and Lease Negotiations

Choosing the right location is critical for the success of your retail business. The perfect location will not only attract customers, but also give your business the exposure it needs to grow. In this chapter, we'll discuss the factors you need to consider before choosing a location for your retail business and how to negotiate a lease that works for you.

FACTORS TO CONSIDER WHEN CHOOSING A LOCATION

When choosing a location for your retail business, there are several factors to consider:

1. Foot Traffic

Foot traffic is the number of people who pass by your store. The higher the foot traffic in a particular location, the greater the chance that people will notice your store and walk in. Look for locations with a high volume of foot traffic, such as shopping malls, busy streets, and popular tourist attractions.

2. Demographics

Consider the demographics of the area you are looking at. Are the people in the area your target market? Will they be interested in your product or service? Make sure the location you choose is in an area where your target market lives or works.

3. Accessibility and Parking

Your location should be easily accessible for your customers, whether they are driving, walking, or using public transportation. Make sure the location has ample parking, whether it's on the street or in a nearby parking lot or garage.

4. Competition

Research the competition in the area and determine if there is room for your retail business. If the area is saturated with similar businesses, it may not be the best location for you. However, if there is a demand for your product or service and little competition, it may be the perfect spot for your business.

NEGOTIATING A LEASE

Once you've found the right location for your retail business, it's time to negotiate a lease with the landlord. Here are some tips to help you negotiate a lease that works for you:

1. Understand your Expenses

Before signing a lease, make sure you understand all of the expenses associated with the location. This includes rent, utilities, maintenance costs, and any other fees that may be required.

2. Negotiate the Rent

Be prepared to negotiate the rent with the landlord. Try to negotiate a lower rent or ask for a rent-free period in the beginning to help you get started.

3. Review the Lease Carefully

Review the lease carefully before signing. Make sure you understand all of the terms and conditions, including the length of the lease, renewal options, and any penalties for breaking the lease early.

4. Seek Legal Advice

If you're unsure about any part of the lease, seek legal advice before signing. A lawyer can help you understand the terms and conditions and make sure you are protected as a tenant.

Choosing the right location for your retail business and negotiating a lease that works for you can be a daunting task. However, with careful consideration and negotiation, you can find the perfect location for your business and set yourself up for success.

Chapter 9: Store Design and Layout

In any retail business, the design and layout of the store are crucial aspects that can impact your sales, customer experience, and overall success. When designing your store, you want to create a layout that is both functional and visually appealing to your customers. Here are some key factors to consider when designing your store:

CUSTOMER FLOW

The flow of your store refers to how customers move through the space. A well-designed store should have a natural flow that leads customers from the entrance to the back of the store, encouraging them to browse and ultimately make a purchase. Here are some tips to optimize customer flow:

- Create a clear entrance - Your store should have a clear and welcoming entrance that draws customers in. Consider adding eye-catching displays or signs that highlight your merchandise.
- Keep the pathway clear - Avoid cluttering the main pathway of your store with displays or fixtures, as this can impede customer flow. Instead, create designated areas for merchandise displays.
- Encourage browsing - Create a layout that encourages customers to browse your merchandise. This can be achieved by placing popular or visually appealing items at the back of the store, which will encourage customers to explore the space.

MERCHANDISE DISPLAY

The way you display your merchandise can also impact your sales. Effective merchandise displays can help showcase your products and entice customers to make a purchase. Consider the following tips when designing your merchandise displays:

- Use eye-catching displays - Create displays that highlight your merchandise in an eye-catching and

creative way. This can be achieved through the use of props, signage, or lighting.
- Create focal points - Use displays to create focal points throughout your store. This draws attention to your best-selling products and encourages customers to explore further.
- Keep displays organized - Make sure that your displays are neat and organized. This will make it easier for customers to identify products and make a purchase.

LIGHTING

Lighting is another crucial aspect of your store's design that can impact the customer experience. Proper lighting can help highlight your merchandise and create a welcoming atmosphere. Consider the following tips when designing your store's lighting:

- Use multiple light sources - Use a combination of natural and artificial light sources to create a balanced and welcoming atmosphere. Consider using different types of lighting fixtures to highlight different areas of your store.
- Adjust the lighting levels - Your lighting levels should be adjustable to

accommodate different times of day or different types of merchandise. For example, if you sell clothing, you may want to have brighter lighting in the dressing rooms to help customers see the fit of the garment.
- Highlight key areas - Use lighting to highlight your merchandise displays and other key areas of your store. This draws attention to these areas and encourages customers to explore further.

By considering customer flow, merchandise displays, and lighting, you can design a store layout that is both functional and visually appealing. Creating a well-designed store can not only improve your sales and customer experience but also set you apart from your competition.

Chapter 10: Inventory Management

Inventory management is a crucial part of any retail business. It involves managing and tracking an organization's stock of products. Effective inventory management will help to ensure that your business has enough products to meet customer demand while minimizing the costs associated with holding inventory. In this chapter, we'll cover a few key subtopics related to inventory management, including determining inventory needs, monitoring and controlling stock levels, and forecasting sales and trends.

SUBCHAPTER 10.1: DETERMINING INVENTORY NEEDS

One of the first steps in effective inventory management is determining the appropriate level of inventory needed to meet customer demand. This requires understanding your sales patterns and forecasting the amount of stock you'll need to have on hand to meet future demand.

One approach to determining inventory needs is to use historical data to track which products sell the most during certain times of the year or during specific promotions. By analyzing sales data over time, you can determine which products are most popular and adjust your inventory levels accordingly.

Another approach is to use point-of-sale (POS) data to track sales in real-time. This can help you adjust inventory levels on the fly to ensure that you always have enough stock on hand.

SUBCHAPTER 10.2: MONITORING AND CONTROLLING STOCK LEVELS

Once you've determined your inventory needs, it's important to regularly monitor and adjust your stock levels. This involves tracking which products are selling well and which products are not, as well as managing stock levels to ensure that you always have enough inventory on hand.

There are several tools that can help you manage your inventory levels. For example, you can use inventory management software to track sales data, forecast demand, and manage your stock levels. This software can also help you automate the reordering process and maintain optimal stock levels to avoid overstocking or understocking.

SUBCHAPTER 10.3: FORECASTING SALES AND TRENDS

Forecasting sales and trends is an important part of inventory management. By predicting future sales patterns, you can adjust your inventory levels to ensure that you always have enough stock on hand to meet demand.

There are several methods that can be used to forecast sales and trends. One method is to use historical sales data to identify patterns and trends. Another method is to use market research to identify emerging trends and adapt your product offerings accordingly. You can also use POS data to track sales in real-time and adjust your inventory levels accordingly.

Effective inventory management requires a balance between meeting customer demand and minimizing costs. By determining inventory needs, monitoring and controlling stock levels, and forecasting sales and trends, you can effectively manage your inventory and improve your business's bottom line.

SUBCHAPTER 10.1: DETERMINING INVENTORY NEEDS

One of the most crucial aspects of running a retail business is to understand and meet the inventory needs. Inventory management helps in ensuring a consistent supply of products to your customers, maximizing sales and profits. However, calculating the right amount of inventory to keep in stock can be quite challenging. Here are some factors you should consider while determining inventory needs:

Product demand

Understanding your product demand is the first step towards determining the inventory needs. It is essential to analyze the sales patterns of a particular product or category over a period. Products that have a steady demand should be stocked adequately, whereas products with unpredictable demand should be stocked in minimal quantities. Keep track of busy periods and identify any trends in sales volume that may be seasonal and account for these trends when determining inventory needs.

Lead time

The lead time is the duration it takes between placing an order and receiving the shipment. It is essential to calculate the lead time for each product to prevent stockouts. If the supplier takes a long time to deliver, you will need to order the products in advance to avoid running out of stock.

Sales history

Monitoring sales history helps retailers project future sales trends, and estimate inventory needs with reasonable accuracy. Analyzing sales, you can identify which products are popular, which are slow-moving, and which are lagging in demand. This data will help you make informed decisions on products you should stock up on and which ones you should reduce to avoid overstocking.

Storage capacity

It is essential to consider your storage capacity when purchasing inventory. It would help if you had enough space to store your products without causing overcrowding, which can hinder access to products or cause damage. Always ensure you have adequate shelving and space available to accommodate new shipments.

Budget and cash flow

In determining inventory levels, you must take into consideration your budget and cash flow. Purchase inventory that aligns with your budget and cash flow, and avoid tying up your cash in inventory that may sit on your shelves for an extended period.

Conclusion

Determining inventory needs is critical as it enables you to make informed decisions regarding the amount and type of products to purchase. By analyzing your sales history, product demand, lead time, storage capacity, and cash flow, you can maintain an efficient and profitable inventory system.

SUBCHAPTER 10.2: MONITORING AND CONTROLLING STOCK LEVELS

Effective inventory management is essential to the success of any retail business. Overstocking can lead to high storage costs, waste, and obsolescence, while understocking can result in lost sales and dissatisfied customers. To avoid both of these scenarios, it is crucial to consistently monitor and control your stock levels. One of the first steps in monitoring your stock levels is to establish an inventory tracking system. This system should include a process for counting and recording all incoming and outgoing stock. You can use a spreadsheet or specialized inventory management software to help you keep track of your inventory. Regularly reviewing your sales data is also important in monitoring and controlling your stock levels. You can use your sales data to identify patterns and trends in the purchasing behavior of your customers. This can help you forecast demand and make informed decisions about stocking levels. To control your stock levels, it is important to establish reorder points for each product. Reorder points are the minimum stock levels at which you should replenish your inventory. Once your stock falls below the reorder point, you should place an order to restock. It is also helpful to establish safety stock levels for each product. Safety stock is the extra stock that you keep on hand to use in case of unexpected demand or delays in restocking. The appropriate amount of safety stock will depend on the lead time and variability in demand for each product. Finally, regularly conducting physical inventory counts can help you identify any discrepancies between your recorded inventory levels and the actual quantity of stock on hand. This will allow you to adjust your inventory tracking system and prevent issues with stock levels in the future. By consistently monitoring and controlling your stock levels, you can ensure that you have the right amount of inventory on hand to meet customer demand without incurring unnecessary costs or losing sales.

SUBCHAPTER 10.3: FORECASTING SALES AND TRENDS

Forecasting sales and trends is an essential part of inventory management in any retail business. It allows you to make informed decisions regarding your inventory and pricing, which can help you optimize your profits and reduce costs. To forecast sales and trends accurately, you need to start with your historical sales data. By analyzing your sales data from previous years, you can identify patterns and trends that can help you make more accurate predictions for the future. There are different methods of forecasting sales and trends, including trend analysis, seasonal analysis, and regression analysis. Trend analysis involves analyzing your historical sales data to identify any long-term trends that may impact your future sales. Seasonal analysis, on the other hand, involves looking at seasonal patterns in your sales data to identify any seasonal trends that may impact your business.

Regression analysis is a more complex method that involves analyzing multiple variables that may impact your sales, such as advertising, promotions, and economic indicators. By analyzing these variables, you can create a statistical model that can help you predict your future sales. It's important to note that forecasting sales and trends is not an exact science. There are many factors that can impact your sales, including competition, new product launches, and changes in consumer behavior. However, by using historical data and analyzing trends, you can make informed predictions that can help you make better decisions for your business. In conclusion, forecasting sales and trends is a crucial part of inventory management in any retail business. By analyzing your historical data and using different forecasting methods, you can make more accurate predictions for the future, which can help you optimize your profits and reduce costs.

Chapter 11: Hiring and Training Staff

One of the most important aspects of running a successful retail business is hiring and training the right staff. Your employees are a direct reflection of your business and they will be responsible for creating a positive experience for your customers. In this chapter, we will discuss the ways in which you can attract and hire top talent in the retail industry, as well as the training and development process to ensure that your employees are equipped with the skills they need to perform their job to the best of their ability.

SUBCHAPTER 11.1: RECRUITING AND INTERVIEWING CANDIDATES

When it comes to recruiting and interviewing candidates, it is important to have a defined process in place to ensure that you are attracting the right people for the job. Here are some tips on how to attract top retail talent:

- Create a detailed job description that outlines the specific requirements and responsibilities of the role.
- Post job listings on relevant job boards, social media, and your company website.

- Encourage employee referrals and incentivize employees for successful referrals.
- Attend job fairs and networking events to meet potential candidates.

Once you have attracted potential candidates for the job, it's time to interview them. Here are some tips for conducting successful interviews:

- Prepare a list of interview questions that are relevant to the job and will help you gauge the candidate's skills and experience.
- Ask behavioral-based questions to get a sense of how the candidate has handled certain situations in the past.
- Take notes during the interview to help with the decision-making process.
- Check references to verify the accuracy of the information provided by the candidate.

SUBCHAPTER 11.2: ONBOARDING AND ORIENTATION

Once you have hired the right candidate, it's important to have a formal onboarding and orientation process to help them get up to speed quickly. Here are some tips on how to effectively onboard and orient new employees:

- Create a detailed training plan that outlines the specific tasks and responsibilities of the job.
- Provide new hires with an employee handbook that outlines company policies and procedures.
- Assign a mentor or buddy to help new hires get acclimated to their role and the company culture.
- Schedule regular check-ins with new hires to ensure they are progressing and have the resources they need to be successful.

SUBCHAPTER 11.3: TRAINING AND DEVELOPMENT

Training and development is an ongoing process in the retail industry. It is important to provide your employees with the skills and tools they need to be successful in their role. Here are some tips for training and developing your retail staff:

- Provide ongoing training on product knowledge, sales techniques, and customer service skills.

- Offer opportunities for employees to attend conferences, workshops, and other training events.
- Provide feedback and coaching to help employees improve their performance.
- Develop career paths and growth opportunities for employees to demonstrate that there is room for advancement within your company.

In conclusion, attracting and retaining top talent is essential to the success of your retail business. By following these tips and implementing effective recruiting, onboarding, and training processes, you can ensure that your employees are equipped with the skills and resources they need to provide excellent customer service and contribute to the growth of your business.

SUBCHAPTER 11.1: RECRUITING AND INTERVIEWING CANDIDATES

Recruiting and interviewing candidates is an essential part of building a successful retail business. The right employees will help you grow your business and provide excellent customer service, while the wrong employees can have the opposite effect.

Here are some tips to help you recruit and interview the best candidates:

Defining Job Descriptions and Requirements

Before you start recruiting, it's essential to have a clear idea of the roles and responsibilities of the job you are filling. Write down what you need someone to do, the skills and experience that are necessary, and the qualifications required. This will help you to create job descriptions and advertisements for the position.

Posting Job Openings

Once you have a clear idea of the job requirements, it's time to post the job opening. You can use job boards, social media, in-store advertising, or local classifieds to advertise the position. Be sure to clearly state the job requirements, duties, and qualifications in your job posting.

Screening Resumes

After you have posted your job opening, you will start to receive resumes from interested candidates. Review the resumes carefully to ensure each candidate meets your qualifications. Consider previous retail experience, education, and achievements when deciding who to bring in for an interview.

Conducting Interviews

The interview process is where you can really get to know your candidates. Prepare a list of questions that will help you determine their experience, skills, and fit for the job. You may want to ask about their previous experience in retail, how they handle difficult customers, and their availability. Consider using a behavioral interview technique where you ask questions that require the candidate to give specific examples of how they have handled certain situations in the past.

Checking References

If you are considering a candidate for the position, it's essential to check their references. This will help you verify the information they provided in their resume and interview. Call previous employers and ask for feedback on the candidate's work history, job duties, attitude, and overall performance.

Making the Hiring Decision

Once you have screened resumes, conducted interviews, and checked references, it's time to make the hiring decision. Consider the candidate's experience, skills, fit for the job, and your overall impression of them. You also need to factor in the candidate's availability and compensation requirements. In conclusion, recruiting and interviewing candidates is an important process to find the best employees for your retail business. Make sure you take the time to define the job requirements, post job openings, screen resumes, conduct interviews, check references, and make the hiring decision that is the best fit for your business.

SUBCHAPTER 11.2: ONBOARDING AND ORIENTATION

Once you have recruited and selected your new hires, it's time to start the onboarding process. Onboarding refers to the process of integrating new employees into your organization and familiarizing them with the company culture, policies, and procedures. Effective onboarding can lead to a smoother transition for new employees and can help them feel more connected and engaged with the company. Orientation, on the other hand, refers to the initial training and introduction to the job. New employees need to understand their roles and responsibilities, as well as the expectations for their performance. Orientation is a crucial step in the onboarding process and should occur as soon as possible after the employee has been hired. Here are some tips for successful onboarding and orientation: 1. Send a welcome email: Before the first day of work, send a personalized welcome email to each new employee. This can include details about the employee's first day, including who they'll be meeting with, what they'll be doing, and what to expect. 2. Assign a mentor or buddy: Assign a mentor or buddy to new hires to help them navigate their first few weeks on the job. This person can answer questions, provide guidance, and serve as a sounding board for any concerns the new employee may have. 3. Provide a clear job description: Make sure each new employee has a clear understanding of their job responsibilities and what is expected of them. This can help them feel more confident and reduce any confusion or anxiety about their role. 4. Develop a training plan: Create a comprehensive training plan that includes both company-wide policies and procedures, as well as job-specific training. New employees should have a clear understanding of how to perform key tasks and how their work fits into the larger goals of the organization. 5. Set up regular check-ins: Schedule regular check-ins with new employees to gauge their progress and offer additional guidance or resources as needed. This can show the employee that you are invested in their success and can help keep them on track. By following these tips, you can ensure that your onboarding and orientation process is successful and sets your new employees up for long-term success at your company. Remember, the onboarding process doesn't end after the first week or two – continue to check in with new hires and offer support and guidance as they acclimate to their new roles.

SUBCHAPTER 11.3: TRAINING AND DEVELOPMENT

One of the keys to running a successful retail business is having a well-trained and motivated staff. Your employees are the face of your business and will play a significant role in shaping your customers' experiences. Therefore, it is important to invest time and resources in their training and development. Training should start on day one and continue throughout an employee's tenure with your company. During the onboarding process, new hires should be given an overview of the company's mission, values, and policies. They should also receive job-specific training that will help them carry out their duties effectively. This can include product knowledge, sales techniques, and customer service skills. Ongoing training and development can take many forms. Consider providing your employees with regular performance feedback and coaching sessions. These can help them identify areas for growth and improvement. You may also want to offer opportunities for cross-training, which can help them develop new skills and become more versatile employees. Another effective way to invest in your staff is to offer professional development opportunities. This can include attending conferences, taking courses or workshops, or pursuing certifications or licenses in their field. By helping your employees grow their skills and knowledge, you are showing them that you value their contributions and are committed to their success. It is also important to create a positive and supportive work environment. Recognize and reward your employees for their hard work and successes, and encourage open communication and collaboration among team members. By fostering a culture of learning and growth, you can help create a motivated and engaged workforce that is committed to your business's success. In conclusion, training and development are essential components of running a successful retail business. By investing in your employees and providing them with the tools and resources they need to succeed, you can create a positive work environment and deliver exceptional customer experiences.

Chapter 12: Marketing and Advertising

Marketing and advertising are essential for any retail business to attract customers and increase foot traffic. In this chapter, we will explore the various strategies and techniques you can use to promote your business and develop a strong brand identity.

DEFINING YOUR TARGET MARKET

The first step in creating a successful marketing strategy is to define your target market. This involves identifying the demographic, psychographic, and behavioral traits of your ideal customer. By understanding who your customers are and what motivates them to buy, you can tailor your marketing efforts to meet their needs.

Some of the factors to consider when defining your target market include age, gender, income level, education level, geographic location, and lifestyle preferences. You can use a combination of market research and customer data analysis to gain insights into your target market.

DEVELOPING A MARKETING STRATEGY

Once you have defined your target market, you can develop a comprehensive marketing strategy that aligns with your business goals and objectives. Your marketing strategy should include a mix of tactics such as advertising, promotions, public relations, and digital marketing.

It is important to set a budget and allocate resources effectively to maximize the impact of your marketing efforts. You should also define key performance indicators (KPIs) to measure the success of your marketing campaigns and make data-driven decisions.

TRADITIONAL ADVERTISING METHODS

Traditional advertising methods such as print ads, billboards, radio ads, and television commercials are still effective in reaching a wide audience. However, they can be expensive and may not be the most efficient use of your marketing budget.

You should consider the pros and cons of each advertising method before deciding which ones to use. For example, print ads can be targeted to specific audiences and have a longer shelf-life, but they may not be as effective in reaching younger demographics.

DIGITAL MARKETING STRATEGIES

Digital marketing has become increasingly important for retailers to reach customers who are spending more time online. Digital marketing methods such as social media marketing, email marketing, content marketing, and search engine optimization (SEO) can be highly effective in driving traffic to your website and increasing conversions.

When developing your digital marketing strategy, it is important to consider your brand messaging, content strategy, and social media presence. You should also measure the success of your digital marketing efforts through metrics such as website traffic, social media engagement, email open rates, and sales.

CONCLUSION

Marketing and advertising are integral components of any successful retail business. By defining your target market, developing a comprehensive marketing strategy, and using both traditional and digital marketing methods, you can attract new customers and increase sales.

Remember to track your results and continually refine your marketing approach to ensure that you are meeting your business objectives.

In the next chapter, we will explore sales techniques that can help you close more deals and increase your bottom line.

SUBCHAPTER 12.1: DEFINING YOUR TARGET MARKET

One of the most important steps in creating an effective marketing strategy is identifying your target market. This refers to the specific group of people who are most likely to be interested in your products or services. Understanding your target market will help you create advertising and promotional campaigns that speak directly to their needs and desires. To define your target market, start by looking at the characteristics of your current customers. Who are they? What are their ages, genders, and income levels? Where do they live, work, and play? What are their interests and hobbies? Once you have a clear idea of your current customer base, you can start to expand your focus to include other potential customers who share similar characteristics. Use market research tools like surveys, questionnaires, and focus groups to gain insights into the preferences and behaviors of your target market. When defining your target market, it's also important to consider the needs and desires of your customers. What problems are they trying to solve with your products or services? What are their pain points and challenges? Understanding these factors will help you create messaging and promotional materials that resonate with your target market. By defining your target market, you'll be better equipped to create marketing campaigns that reach the right people, through the right channels, at the right times. This will help you maximize your marketing ROI and drive more sales and revenue for your business.

SUBCHAPTER 12.2: DEVELOPING A MARKETING STRATEGY

Once you have defined your target market, it's important to develop a marketing strategy that will effectively reach and engage that audience. A well-crafted marketing strategy can help you attract new customers, build brand awareness, and increase sales. Here are some steps to follow when developing your marketing strategy: 1. Identify Your Unique Selling Proposition (USP): Your USP is what sets your business apart from the competition. It should be a clear and compelling message that communicates the value of your product or service to your target audience. 2. Define Your Marketing Goals: Determine what you want to achieve with your marketing efforts. This could be anything from increasing website traffic to boosting sales. Make sure your goals are specific, measurable, and realistic. 3. Conduct a Market Analysis: It's important to understand the current market trends and your competition. Conduct research to identify what your competitors are doing and what their strengths and weaknesses are. Use this information to inform your marketing strategy. 4. Choose Your Marketing Channels: Consider which marketing channels will be the most effective in reaching your target audience. This could include social media, email marketing, paid advertising, and more. 5. Develop Your Marketing Tactics: Once you've identified your channels, develop specific tactics for each one. For example, if you're focusing on social media, you might develop a content calendar and schedule regular posts. 6. Set Your Marketing Budget: Determine how much you can realistically spend on marketing and allocate your budget accordingly. Make sure to track your spending and adjust your strategy as needed. 7. Monitor Your Results: It's important to track your marketing metrics to determine what's working and what's not. Use this data to refine your strategy and optimize your marketing efforts. Remember, a successful marketing strategy requires ongoing effort and adjustment. Don't be afraid to experiment with new tactics and adjust your approach as needed to achieve your marketing goals.

SUBCHAPTER 12.3: TRADITIONAL ADVERTISING METHODS

Despite the ever-increasing popularity of digital marketing, traditional advertising methods still have a significant role to play in promoting your retail business. These methods include both print and broadcast advertising and can be highly effective in driving traffic to your store and boosting sales. Some of the most common traditional advertising methods include:

Newspaper Ads

Newspaper advertisements are a staple of traditional marketing and can be an extremely cost-effective way to reach potential customers. With a well-crafted ad and a targeted approach to placement, you can grab the attention of local readers and generate interest in your store.

Direct Mail

Direct mail campaigns can be an effective way to reach customers in your local area or even further afield. By targeting specific demographics through mailing lists, you can increase the relevancy and effectiveness of your ads and drive more traffic to your store.

Radio Ads

Radio advertising can be an effective means of reaching a broad audience and can be a particularly powerful tool for promoting time-sensitive events or promotions. By crafting a well-written ad and targeting stations with listeners who fit your target demographic, you can generate increased interest in your store and boost sales.

TV Ads

While TV advertising can be expensive, it can also be an incredibly powerful way to promote your retail business. By crafting an interesting and attention-grabbing ad and targeting the right network and time slots, you can reach a wide audience and generate significant interest in your store. It's important to note that finding the right traditional advertising mix for your business will depend on a variety of factors, including your budget, target audience, and local market conditions. That said, by experimenting with different methods and closely tracking your results, you can develop a powerful advertising strategy that drives traffic to your store and boosts sales.

SUBCHAPTER 12.4: DIGITAL MARKETING STRATEGIES

In today's digital age, it's more important than ever for retailers to have a strong online presence and employ digital marketing strategies to reach their target audience. Here are some effective digital marketing strategies that retailers can use to drive traffic and increase sales:

Social Media Marketing:

Social media is a powerful tool that can help retailers connect with their customers and build brand awareness. Retailers can use platforms like Facebook, Instagram, Twitter, and LinkedIn to promote their products, share valuable content, and engage with their followers.

Email Marketing:

Email marketing is a cost-effective way for retailers to reach their customers directly and promote their products. Retailers can use email campaigns to promote new products, offer discounts, and share valuable content that provides value to their subscribers.

Content Marketing:

Content marketing is all about creating high-quality and valuable content that educates, entertains, or informs your target audience. Retailers can use blog posts, videos, infographics, and other forms of content to attract and engage potential customers.

Search Engine Optimization (SEO):

SEO is the process of optimizing your website and content to rank higher in search engine results pages. Retailers can use SEO to increase their visibility online and attract more organic traffic to their website.

Pay-Per-Click (PPC) Advertising:

PPC advertising is a form of online advertising where retailers pay for each click on their ads. Retailers can use platforms like Google Ads and Facebook Ads to reach their target audience and promote their products.

Affiliate Marketing:

Affiliate marketing is a popular marketing strategy where retailers partner with other websites or influencers to promote their products. Retailers pay these partners a commission for each sale that they generate. Implementing a digital marketing strategy can be overwhelming, but it's important for retailers to stay competitive in today's ever-changing retail landscape. By leveraging digital marketing strategies like social media, email marketing, content marketing, SEO, PPC advertising, and affiliate marketing, retailers can drive traffic, increase sales, and build stronger relationships with their customers.

Chapter 13: Sales Techniques

As a retail business owner, your ultimate goal is to drive sales and increase revenue. This requires an understanding of effective sales techniques, which can help you attract customers, improve their experiences, and ultimately lead to more sales. In this chapter, we will explore some key sales techniques that every retail business owner should be familiar with.

SUBCHAPTER 13.1: SALES SKILLS AND STRATEGIES

One of the most essential sales skills is the ability to listen to your customers. When prospective customers enter your store, pay attention to their needs and preferences, and engage with them in a friendly, helpful manner. Ask questions to understand their shopping goals and offer personalized recommendations based on their responses. Remember, every customer is unique and may require a different approach.

Another important sales technique is to focus on the value of your products. As opposed to simply highlighting the features and specs, emphasize the ways in which your products can solve a problem or enhance your customer's life. This is particularly effective when it comes to selling higher-priced or luxury items.

SUBCHAPTER 13.2: HANDLING CUSTOMER COMPLAINTS AND CHALLENGES

No matter how excellent your products and customer service are, it is inevitable that you will encounter customer complaints and challenges. Don't view these as setbacks, but rather opportunities to address concerns and improve your overall business. When handling a complaint, be sure to listen actively, apologize if necessary, and work towards finding a solution that works for both parties.

Another strategy for dealing with customer complaints is to empower your employees to take ownership of the problem. Encourage them to use their judgment and come up with creative solutions on the spot, rather than always escalating a problem to management. This not only speeds up the resolution process but also shows your customers that you value them and their feedback.

SUBCHAPTER 13.3: UPSELLING AND CROSS-SELLING TECHNIQUES

Upselling and cross-selling are both strategies to drive revenue by increasing the average sale value. Upselling involves offering a more expensive alternative to the product or service that the customer is considering, while cross-selling involves suggesting complementary or related products.

A few effective techniques for upselling include offering a premium version of the product, highlighting the added features that come with the more expensive option, and emphasizing how the higher-priced option will solve the customer's problems more effectively.

When it comes to cross-selling, it's important to suggest products that complement the customer's current purchase and will truly enhance their experience. This can be achieved by knowing your product inventory very well and identifying products that are frequently purchased together or are relevant to a customer's specific needs.

CONCLUSION

By utilizing these sales techniques, you can ensure that your retail business not only attracts customers but also drives sales and revenue. Remember to listen to your customers, focus on the value of your products, handle complaints effectively, and use upselling and cross-selling techniques wisely. By doing so, you can build a loyal customer base and enhance your business's reputation.

SUBCHAPTER 13.1: SALES SKILLS AND STRATEGIES

In any retail business, sales are the lifeblood of the operation. To be successful, it is crucial to have skilled salespeople who can close deals and help customers find the products they need. In this subchapter, we'll discuss some essential sales skills and strategies that can help your team excel.

Listening Skills

One of the most crucial skills for a salesperson to have is the ability to listen actively. Listening is key to understanding a customer's needs and preferences. Sales reps who can ask good questions and then listen carefully to the answers can tailor their product recommendations to the customer's specific needs, making it more likely that they will make a purchase.

Product Knowledge

Of course, to make good product recommendations, your sales team needs to know your inventory inside and out. Encourage your team to study and learn about the products you offer - the more they know, the more confidently they can speak to customers.

Customer Empathy

Another critical trait of top salespeople is the ability to empathize with customers. Having empathy means that the sales rep can put themselves in the customer's shoes and understand their perspective. Empathetic sales staff can build rapport with customers and make them feel more comfortable - a crucial factor in making a sale.

Effective Communication

Clear and effective communication is essential in sales. Salespeople must be able to explain the benefits of a product in a way that resonates with the customer, using language that is easy to understand. They should avoid using jargon or technical terms that might confuse or intimidate customers.

Selling Techniques

There are many different techniques that salespeople can use to close deals and encourage purchases. Some common approaches include upselling (offering customers a more expensive version of the product they are considering), cross-selling (suggesting complementary products that the customer might be interested in), and scarcity tactics (emphasizing limited product availability to encourage customers to buy now).

Closing the Deal

At the end of the day, the goal of every sales interaction is to close the deal and make a sale. Your sales team should know how to recognize buying signals, ask for the sale at the right time, and handle objections that might arise. With proper training and guidance, your sales team can become experts at closing the deal and driving revenue for your business.

By teaching your sales staff these essential skills and strategies, you can help them become top performers who can drive business growth for your retail operation.

SUBCHAPTER 13.2: HANDLING CUSTOMER COMPLAINTS AND CHALLENGES

No matter how well-run a retail business is, there will always be customer complaints and challenges. It's essential to handle those situations appropriately to protect your store's reputation, maintain customer satisfaction, and avoid losing revenue. One vital aspect of handling customer complaints is to acknowledge the issue promptly. Always listen to customer grievances empathetically, showing concern and understanding for their situation. Your response can significantly affect the outcome of the situation. If you appear uninterested or dismissive, it will only escalate the problem. Take responsibility for the situation, apologize for the inconvenience and work towards finding a solution that meets their expectations while remaining realistic. Keep communication channels open throughout the process, maintaining transparency and keeping the customer informed about what you are doing to resolve the issue. Handling customer challenges is a different beast entirely but is equally crucial to preserve customer satisfaction levels. We are human, and sometimes human error occurs in our daily operations, mistakes happen, and unforeseeable situations arise. When dealing with customer challenges, it is vital to take a proactive approach, anticipate any potential issues, and stop them before they happen. Effective processes, procedures, and training can mitigate the risks of possible situations that can arise. Remember, it costs more to attract new customers than to retain existing ones, so prioritizing customer satisfaction and handling any issues quickly and efficiently should be a top priority in any retail business.

Chapter 14: Managing Business Finances

One of the crucial aspects of running a retail business is managing your finances properly. Without proper management, your business may struggle to remain profitable and sustainable. In this chapter, we will discuss various strategies and techniques to help you efficiently manage your business's finances.

BUDGETING AND FORECASTING

Creating a budget is one of the first steps towards managing your business's finances. A budget will help you understand your cash flow, expenses, and revenue forecasts. In turn, this will enable you to make informed decisions about important areas of your business such as marketing, hiring, inventory management, etc.

When creating a budget, you should take the following steps:

- Identify all the sources of revenue for your business
- List all your fixed and variable expenses
- Determine your break-even point
- Set financial targets and goals
- Monitor and adjust your budget regularly

Once you have created a budget, you should regularly review it and make necessary adjustments. This will ensure that you're staying on track with your financial goals and objectives.

BOOKKEEPING AND ACCOUNTING

Another important aspect of managing your business's finances is proper bookkeeping and accounting. You need to keep track of all your financial transactions, such as sales, expenses, payables, and receivables. This will help you maintain an accurate financial record of your business.

Here are some tips for effective bookkeeping and accounting:

- Use accounting software to simplify record-keeping

- Maintain an organized filing system for receipts and invoices
- Reconcile bank statements on a regular basis
- Separate personal and business finances
- Track inventory levels and costs

By keeping detailed and accurate financial records, you will be better equipped to make informed financial decisions for your business.

FINANCIAL PERFORMANCE ANALYSIS

Regularly analyzing your business's financial performance is crucial to its success. With financial analysis, you can identify which areas of your business are performing well and which areas need improvement.

Here are some of the key metrics you should track:

- Gross profit margin
- Net profit margin
- Inventory turnover ratio
- Debt-to-equity ratio
- Return on investment (ROI)

Tracking these metrics will help you assess your business's overall financial health, profitability, and growth potential. By identifying areas that need improvement, you can take corrective actions to ensure your business remains financially sustainable.

CONCLUSION

Managing your business's finances is critical to its success and sustainability. By creating a budget, maintaining accurate financial records, and regularly analyzing your financial performance, you can make informed decisions that will help grow your business.

SUBCHAPTER 14.1: BUDGETING AND FORECASTING

As a retail business owner, effective budgeting and forecasting are essential for your long-term success. Budgeting involves the process of planning how you will allocate your available resources in order to achieve your goals. Forecasting, on the other hand, involves predicting your future income and expenses based on historical data and market trends. There are several steps you can take to create a budget for your retail business. Firstly, calculate your total revenue, taking into account all sources of income including sales, financing, and investments. Next, identify all your expenses, including fixed costs such as rent, utilities, and salaries, as well as variable expenses, such as marketing and inventory costs. By subtracting your total expenses from your total revenue, you can determine your net profit. Once you have an idea of your budget, you should also create a financial forecast based on predicted future sales and expenses. This can help you identify potential issues before they arise and make informed decisions about future investments and expansions. You can base your forecast on a variety of factors, including previous sales data, seasonal trends, and changes in the marketplace. It's important to regularly monitor your budget and forecast to ensure that you are on track to meet your goals. Make sure to review your financial statements on a regular basis, making adjustments as necessary to stay within your budget and adapt to changes in the market. By effectively budgeting and forecasting, you will be able to identify and mitigate financial risks and position your retail business for long-term success.

SUBCHAPTER 14.2: BOOKKEEPING AND ACCOUNTING

Bookkeeping and accounting are crucial components of managing the finances of a retail business. Proper bookkeeping ensures that you have an accurate record of your financial transactions, and accounting helps you understand the financial performance of your business. To ensure effective bookkeeping, consider hiring an experienced accountant who can help you manage your books, advise you on financial strategies, and prepare financial statements. Alternatively, you can use software to manage your books, such as QuickBooks and Xero. There are several types of financial statements that you need to prepare, including the balance sheet, income statement, and cash flow statement. The balance sheet reflects the assets, liabilities, and equity of the business at a specific point in time. The income statement shows the revenue, expenses, and net income or loss for a period. The cash flow statement outlines the inflows and outflows of cash and cash equivalents in a period. It's important to keep track of all your financial transactions, including sales, expenses, payroll, and inventory. You should reconcile your books with your bank statements regularly to ensure accuracy. You can also use accounting software to automate processes such as invoicing, payroll, and payments. Proper bookkeeping and accounting not only ensure your financial records are accurate but also help you make informed business decisions based on financial analysis. It's crucial to monitor your financial statements regularly and compare them with industry benchmarks to identify areas for improvement and opportunities for growth. In conclusion, bookkeeping and accounting are essential for the success of your retail business. Whether you hire an accountant or use software, ensure that you have accurate records of your financial transactions and regularly analyze your financial statements to make informed decisions.

SUBCHAPTER 14.3: FINANCIAL PERFORMANCE ANALYSIS

As a retail business owner, it's crucial to regularly analyze your company's financial performance. This will help you make informed decisions about your business's future and ensure that your company is profitable. There are several ways to analyze your retail business's financial performance. One way is to use financial ratios, which are calculations that compare different financial metrics to provide insight into your company's financial health. One important financial ratio is the gross profit margin. This ratio measures the percentage of sales revenue that remains after the cost of goods sold is subtracted. A high gross profit margin indicates that your business is pricing its products or services effectively and managing its costs well. Another financial ratio is the return on investment (ROI), which measures how much profit your business generates relative to its total capital investments. A high ROI indicates that your business is generating a strong return on the money invested in it. In addition to financial ratios, it's important to review other financial metrics, such as sales revenue, net income, and cash flow. By analyzing these metrics, you can identify areas of your business that are performing well and areas that may need improvement. It's also critical to monitor your business's expenses regularly. By closely tracking your expenses, you can identify opportunities to reduce costs and improve your business's profitability. Overall, regularly analyzing your retail business's financial performance can help you make informed decisions, identify trends, and ensure that your business remains profitable and successful in the long-term.

Chapter 15: Scaling Your Business

Scaling a business means to grow it in a manageable way. Business owners are always looking for ways to expand and grow their customer base. Below are some strategies that can help you scale your retail business.

SUBCHAPTER 15.1: GROWING YOUR CUSTOMER BASE

The first step to scaling your retail business is to increase your customer base. Here are some ways you can do that:

- Run Promotions: One of the simplest ways to get new customers is to run promotions. Offer deals, discounts, and freebies to attract new customers to your store.
- Referral Program: Word of mouth is a powerful marketing tool. Offer your existing customers a discount or reward for referring new customers to your store.
- Use Social Media: Social media is a great way to attract new customers. Use platforms like Facebook, Twitter, and Instagram to promote your store and engage with potential customers.
- Partner with Other Businesses: Partnering with other businesses can help you reach new customers. Look for opportunities to collaborate with other businesses in your area.
- Expand Your Product Line: Adding new products to your store can also help you attract new customers. Conduct market research to determine

what types of products your customers are interested in.

SUBCHAPTER 15.2: EXPANDING YOUR PRODUCT OR SERVICE OFFERINGS

Once you have a solid customer base, the next step is to expand your product or service offerings. Here are some ways you can do that:

- Diversify Your Product Line: Offer a wider range of products to appeal to more customers. Consider adding complementary products to your existing line.
- Services: Adding services to your store can also help you stand out from your competitors. For example, if you own a clothing store, you could offer tailoring or alterations services.
- Online Sales: Expanding your sales to online platforms can also help you grow your customer base. Consider building an online store or selling your products on established online marketplaces.

SUBCHAPTER 15.3: FRANCHISING AND LICENSING

If you have a successful business model, you can consider franchising or licensing it to other entrepreneurs. This can help you expand your business quickly and with less capital investment. Here are some things to consider before franchising or licensing:

- Brand Strength: Make sure your brand is strong enough to support a franchise model.
- Legal Considerations: There are legal requirements involved in franchising or licensing a business. Make sure you consult with an attorney to ensure compliance with the law.
- Training: You need to develop a comprehensive training program to ensure franchisees or licensees can follow your business model successfully.
- Fees and Royalties: Make sure you set appropriate fees and royalties for your franchise or license agreements.

Scaling a retail business requires careful planning, but by expanding your customer base, product or service offerings, and exploring franchising and licensing options, you can successfully grow your business.

SUBCHAPTER 15.1: GROWING YOUR CUSTOMER BASE

Growing your customer base is crucial to the success and longevity of your retail business. The more customers you have, the more sales and profits you can generate. Here are some strategies to help you grow your customer base:

1. Focus on Customer Service

Providing excellent customer service should be a top priority for your business. When customers have a positive experience with your company, they are more likely to recommend you to others and become repeat customers themselves. Train your employees to be friendly, attentive and knowledgeable about your products or services.

2. Offer Promotions and Discounts

Promotions and discounts are a great way to attract new customers to your business. Offer a discount for first-time customers or create a loyalty program that rewards repeat business. Host sales events and offer exclusive deals to your email subscribers to entice them to make a purchase.

3. Use Social Media Marketing

Social media can be a powerful tool for reaching new customers and promoting your business. Determine which platforms your target audience uses and create engaging content that resonates with them. Offer exclusive promotions for your social media followers and encourage them to share your content with their networks.

4. Attend Networking Events

Attending networking events can help increase your visibility and introduce you to potential customers. Join local business associations or attend industry conferences to connect with other business owners and potential partners. Make sure to bring business cards and be prepared to talk about your business.

5. Collect Customer Feedback

Asking for and implementing customer feedback can help you improve your business and attract new customers. Encourage customers to leave reviews online and use this feedback to address any issues or make changes to your products or services. By showing potential customers that you value and listen to customer feedback, you can earn their trust and business. By implementing these strategies, you can steadily grow your customer base and take your retail business to new heights. Remember, acquiring new customers takes time and effort, but the payoff can be well worth it.

SUBCHAPTER 15.2: EXPANDING YOUR PRODUCT OR SERVICE OFFERINGS

Expanding your product or service offerings is a crucial aspect of scaling your retail business. It is important to keep your offerings fresh and exciting to continue to attract and retain customers. Here are some strategies you can use to expand your offerings:

1. Analyze Your Current Offerings

Before expanding, it is important to analyze your current offerings. Determine which products or services are selling well and which ones are not. Look at customer feedback to identify any pain points or gaps in your current offerings. This information will help you determine which areas to focus on when expanding.

2. Research Trends and Competitors

Before introducing new products or services, it is important to research industry trends and see what your competitors are offering. Look for gaps in the market that you can fill with unique and innovative offerings. This can help you differentiate your business from competitors and attract new customers.

3. Modify Current Offerings

You don't necessarily need to introduce completely new offerings to expand. You can modify your existing offerings to appeal to new customers or expand into new markets. For example, if you own a clothing store, you can add plus-size options to your current lineup to appeal to a wider customer base.

4. Consider Bundling

Bundling can be a great way to expand your offerings while increasing sales. You can bundle related products or services together at a discounted price to encourage customers to buy more. For example, a coffee shop can bundle a sandwich and a drink together for a discounted price.

5. Partner with Other Businesses

Partnering with other businesses can be a great way to expand your offerings and reach new customers. Look for complementary businesses that you can partner with to offer bundled packages or joint promotions. For example, a boutique clothing store may partner with a local jewelry store to offer a discount when customers purchase items from both stores.

6. Keep Your Brand Image Consistent

It's important to maintain your brand image when expanding your offerings. Make sure any new products or services you introduce are in line with your brand and appeal to your target market. This will help maintain customer loyalty and ensure a consistent customer experience across all offerings. Expanding your product or service offerings can help you reach new customers, increase sales, and differentiate yourself from competitors. By analyzing your current offerings, researching trends and competitors, modifying current offerings, bundling, partnering with other businesses, and keeping your brand image consistent, you can successfully expand your offerings.

SUBCHAPTER 15.3: FRANCHISING AND LICENSING

Franchising or licensing can be a great way to expand your business without the risks associated with opening a brand new location. Both franchising and licensing are legal arrangements that allow a business owner to allow another entity to operate under their brand name. Franchising involves the business owner granting the franchisee the right to use their brand name, products or services, and business model. The franchisee then operates the business using the rules set by the franchisor. The franchisor generally provides initial training and ongoing support to the franchisee. Licensing, on the other hand, is an agreement that allows a business owner to permit another party to use their intellectual property, such as patents, trademarks, or copyrights. This is often done by manufacturers who grant licenses to other businesses to produce and sell their products under their brand name. There are many benefits to franchising or licensing your business. For one, it allows you to expand your market share without investing in new locations or employees. Additionally, franchisees and licensees are responsible for their own start-up costs, which can significantly reduce your financial risk. However, there are also some downsides to franchising or licensing your business. You must be prepared to give up a certain amount of control over your business when you enter into these types of agreements. You also need to be prepared to provide ongoing support and training to your franchisees or licensees. Finally, there may be legal and regulatory requirements that vary by state or country. If you are considering franchising or licensing your business, it is important to seek out legal and financial advice before making any decisions. A qualified attorney or accountant can help you understand the pros and cons of these options and how they can impact your business.

Chapter 16: Conclusion and Next Steps

Congratulations on reaching the end of this book, "Retail Businesses Made Easy"! We hope the information presented here has been valuable to you in starting or growing your own retail business.

By now, you should have a solid understanding of what it takes to start and run a successful retail business. From choosing the right business idea, to creating a business plan, to hiring and training staff, to developing effective marketing and sales strategies, this book has covered all the key topics you need to know.

Now that you have the knowledge, it's time to take action. Use the information in this book to create a roadmap for your own retail business success. Remember, while knowledge is important, it's action that leads to results.

NEXT STEPS

So, what should you do next? Here are some suggested steps to help you get started:

- Refine your business idea: Take some time to research your niche and target market to ensure that your business idea is as solid as possible.
- Create a comprehensive business plan: Use the guidelines provided in this book to develop a detailed plan for your business that includes financial projections, marketing strategies, and more.
- Fund your business: Explore financing options such as loans, grants, and crowdfunding to help get your business off the ground.
- Register your business: Follow the steps outlined in Chapter 6 to register your business with the necessary governmental agencies.
- Design your store layout: Use the tips provided in Chapter 9 to create a welcoming, strategically planned store layout that promotes sales.
- Manage your inventory: Take the advice presented in Chapter 10 to ensure that you're always stocked with

the right products and quantities to meet customer demand.
- Hire and train staff: Use the guidelines presented in Chapter 11 to recruit, interview, and train reliable employees who will represent your brand well to customers.
- Develop a marketing strategy: Follow the steps in Chapter 12 to develop comprehensive marketing strategies that utilize both traditional and digital methods to reach your target audience.
- Refine your sales techniques: Use the tips in Chapter 13 to develop a sales strategy that focuses on building relationships with customers and handling complaints with grace and professionalism.
- Manage your finances: Use the tools outlined in Chapter 14 to stay on top of your business finances and ensure your profitability.
- Scale your business: Use the advice in Chapter 15 to grow your customer base, expand your product or service offerings, or explore franchising or licensing opportunities.

Remember, running a successful retail business takes time, effort, dedication, and persistence. However, armed with the information provided in this book, you're well on your way to achieving your goals!

Best of luck on your journey, and we wish you all the best in your retail business endeavors!

www.ingramcontent.com/pod-product-compliance
Lightning Source LLC
Chambersburg PA
CBHW030443220526
45464CB00006B/2399